Souvenir Guide

Contents

Produced exclusively for SCMG Enterprises Ltd
By Carlton Books Ltd, 20 Mortimer Street, London W1T 3JW

National Railway Museum logo © SCMG and designs © SCMG.
Every purchase supports the museum. www.nrm.org.uk

Text written by Tony Streeter.

ISBN 978-1-78097-464-4

Printed in Dubai.

Front cover image: Flying Scotsman, photographed in 2011 by
Lynn Patrick.
Page 1: Flying Scotsman Empire Exhibition Wembley 1924, Fig. 3.
E2013.507.173

Foreword

A very warm welcome to the world's greatest railway museum. We're the custodians of over 1 million incredible objects spanning 300 years of unique railway history. Whether you've travelled to us from within the UK or from overseas, I hope this book will inspire you to discover more about railways.

The story of railways is an important one to tell. From the Industrial Revolution to the present day, they have shaped all our lives – from the food we eat, to the goods we buy and our connections with friends, family and work. We are here to tell this story, brought to life through unique gallery spaces, learning experiences and a changing programme of special events and exhibitions. It's a story that continues into the future as railways enjoy a huge renaissance. Passenger numbers in the UK are back to the peak of the 1920s and are forecast to grow further. New high speed lines link London with the Continent and there are hotly debated plans for expansion north with High Speed Two (HS2).

The National Railway Museum is home to this history: giant halls full of railway legends, powerful engines and glamorous carriages. In the Great Hall marvel at the steam world-record-breaking Mallard and climb onboard the only bullet train outside Japan. Soak up the nostalgic atmosphere of our Station Hall where you can experience station working life and the world's finest collection of royal carriages including Queen Victoria's favourite carriage. Don't miss the Warehouse, home to a treasure trove of fascinating objects, including the bullion box from the Great Gold Robbery of 1855.

I hope you will enjoy your journey around the museum and will come back to discover how this epic story unfolds.

Paul Kirkman

Paul Kirkman
Director, National Railway Museum

Introduction

The National Railway Museum is home to the world's greatest railway collection. Our halls are a treasure trove telling the story of Britain's railway successes – and some dead-ends too. Here, you can learn how railways have shaped our lives.

RIGHT
View overlooking Great Hall, with the locomotives in our collection gathered around the turntable.

BELOW
Carriages line the platforms in the Station Hall.

Britain gave railways to the world, and fortunately in the 19th century the enlightened policies of some individuals and companies meant irreplaceable items from the pioneering days survived to be wondered at by a modern audience. An official collecting policy in later years added key examples of milestones in railway history, from large objects down to everyday minutiae such as the tickets that would have filled passengers' pockets.

Even our site is full of history. The inviting exhibition space that is now the Great Hall was once a part of the dirty, smoky York North sheds where workers laboriously prepared giant steam locomotives to pull main line trains. Station Hall, today home to our unrivalled collection of royal train carriages, was previously a goods depot where trains came to be loaded and unloaded. Before 1962, Britain's railways were 'common carriers', which meant they were required by law to carry any goods – even hazardous ones.

However, the museum is not only about preserving the past. Our aim is to interpret the technological, social, cultural and political impact of railways – and we collect to reflect both historical and contemporary stories.

Nearly 60 locomotives, carriages and wagons are displayed at York alone, with others at our site at Shildon in County Durham, and yet more on loan to other museums and railways around the country. In the Search Engine archive you can consult 20,000 books and 750,000 engineering drawings, the correspondence of George and Robert Stephenson, a collection of paintings of railway engineer Timothy Hackworth and family, and sound archives that include tapes by Oscar-winning sound recordist Peter Handford. In addition, our collection includes 12,000 posters and 1.75 million photographs.

York has long been a railway centre, its connection to the world's first mass transport dating back to the days of the Victorian 'free for all' in railway building that resulted in more than 100 private companies opening often competing lines. Back then, the famous Railway King, George Hudson, boasted that he would make all railways come to this city – an exaggeration,

but one demonstrating just how important York was. It still is today, decades after the private companies were at first grouped together by government decree in 1923, then nationalised in 1948, and then privatised again in the 1990s.

In 1975, when the National Railway Museum opened, we became the first national museum outside London. By that point York already had a long tradition of housing a railway museum; the first was opened in 1928 by the London & North Eastern Railway (LNER), successor to the world's first public railway to use steam locomotives, the Stockton & Darlington Railway (S&DR). The work of commercial organisations like the LNER built on the early efforts of the Patent Office and later the Science Museum: the National Railway Museum is part of the Science Museum Group, the world's biggest alliance of national science museums. Artefacts of worldwide importance saved by the Patent Office include Stephenson's Rocket, and the early locomotives Agenoria and Puffing Billy.

The National Railway Museum welcomes hundreds of thousands of visitors to York and Shildon every year. Shildon is an important historic railway site, for this is where passengers started their journey in 1825 when the Stephenson engine Locomotion pulled the S&DR's opening train. However, our telling of Britain's railway story goes much further than simply running the two museum sites.

National collection locomotives operate at preserved railways and on the country's main lines, ensuring their wide exposure and display to the public. Our active participation in the preservation of Britain's railway history also includes undertaking conservation of artefacts at our York site and in partnership with specialist contractors; this ranges from locomotive restoration to the preservation of documents and paintings. Visitors to York can see for themselves some of the activity from the public balcony overlooking the Workshop where we can undertake work on locomotives, carriages, wagons and other large exhibits.

History never stands still, and so the museum must constantly move forward in order to reflect the ever-changing nature of railways in Britain and across the world. We continue to collect and to develop new displays, and we have ambitious plans to develop our York site.

In the pages that follow we present more than 60 highlights from our collection. They are arranged in chronological order to illustrate the development of the railways, from an early section of track to high speed trains. They also show the range of objects we have at the museum. Divided into five sections they cover everything from record-breaking locomotives like Flying Scotsman and Mallard to curiosities such as the model of a carriage where a murder was committed, and a boot used by railway workers in vans transporting explosives during the First World War.

Origins of the Railways

Travel before railways was slow. If you could afford it, you might move at the speed of a horse. If not, you had to walk.

Yet the railways were not born for transporting people, but for industry. The first railroads were simple wooden tracks, built in the 16th century to move tubs of coal in mines. By the early 1700s, iron rails were used too. With Thomas Newcomen's invention of a pumping engine in 1712 and later improvements by engineers such as James Watt, stationary steam engines became widely adopted and were primarily used for pumping water, driving machinery and winding cables. Then in 1803 Cornish inventor Richard Trevithick ran the first steam locomotive on rails, at Penydarren Ironworks in Wales. His locomotive successfully pulled 10 tons of iron, with people, along the Merthyr Tramroad.

Soon, mine owners in northeast England, keen to reduce the high costs of moving coal by horse, began to employ engineers to design and build steam-operated railways. In 1825, the world's first public railway to use steam locomotives began services between Stockton and Darlington. The first train was pulled by Locomotion, built in Newcastle-upon-Tyne by a company set up by the father and son railway pioneers, George and Robert Stephenson. The price of coal in Stockton dropped from 18 shillings per ton to 8 shillings 6 pence after the railway opened.

Four years after that, the Stephensons' Rocket triumphed in the Rainhill Trials, a competition held to choose locomotives for the Liverpool & Manchester Railway (L&MR). It opened in 1830 and Rocket's innovative design set the template used for locomotives until the end of steam in the 1960s.

Within a decade, the foundations had been laid for Britain's transport backbone, made possible by a technology that would ultimately transform the world.

LEFT
Railways brought new dangers. This is Parkside, where Liverpool's Member of Parliament William Huskisson was hit by Stephenson's Rocket on 15 September 1830, at the opening of the L&MR. He died later that day.

1979-8250

ABOVE

This book by John Curr dates from 1797 and is the earliest printed account of a railway. It describes an industrial 'plateway' and pre-dates the use of locomotives.

1997-179

LEFT

Rails have been laid in mines for centuries. This wooden track from Groverake coal mine in County Durham is typical of the tramways where wagons were moved by horses or people.

1976-7021

1829

The Rastrick Notebook

This is John Rastrick's notebook from the Rainhill Trials, where the Stephensons won the competition to provide locomotives for the world's first inter-city route, the Liverpool & Manchester Railway. Rastrick was one of the three judges. Ironically, Rocket, the locomotive that won the trials, rendered Rastrick's own locomotive Agenoria outdated.

1945-108

1804

Model steam locomotive
Sans Pareil

This model has multiple cylinders and is a prototype for all the fossil-fuel powered transport that followed. It might have been built by either of the famous early locomotive pioneers Timothy Hackworth or Richard Trevithick, or possibly by clockmaker William West, who is known to have built models for Trevithick.

2006-7463

1829

Agenoria

One of the world's oldest locomotives, Agenoria is a close relative of the first locomotive to run in the USA, the Stourbridge Lion of 1828. The company of Foster, Rastrick built only four locomotives, and three went to the Delaware and Hudson Canal Company. The remaining one was Agenoria, which takes its name from a Roman Goddess. It was supplied to Staffordshire's Shutt End Colliery where it pulled coal wagons for 35 years.

1884-92

Expansion and Impact

Railways quickly transformed people's lives. Rapid growth brought new challenges which led to innovations and improvements in safety and efficiency.

How do you create a safe, useable schedule when there is no unified time? Or ensure you have been paid for the journeys passengers make? How do people navigate themselves around an ever more comprehensive and complicated system?

Answers came quickly as railways developed increasingly sophisticated operating systems and inventors devised the technologies that enabled them to work. 'Railway time' took over from local time zones, machines were developed to replace the laborious process of having to write out tickets, and a household name was launched when the comprehensive Bradshaw's Railway Companion timetable was published for the first time.

By the end of the 1830s, many of Britain's key cities were already connected. The following decade brought Railway Mania as rival companies fought to build more lines, and businessmen and investors tried to get rich quick. Entrepreneurs, like York's George Hudson, came to mastermind large business empires, but could lose them, too, when stock markets crashed.

Trains unlocked an age of mass travel that would have previously been impossible, and every class of society saw the benefits. Things that needed to be distributed quickly such as fresh food, or newspapers, could be moved long distances in a timely manner for the first time. Queen Victoria adopted the new technology early, making her first journey in 1842.

It wasn't only individual lives that were transformed. The industrial might that efficient transport unleashed fuelled the growth of cities and helped Britain become the world's most powerful nation. Export markets were created too, as other countries tried to catch up with the UK's success and railways facilitated the expansion of empire.

RIGHT
Bradshaw's Railway Companion became the leading timetable. It started as an extremely slim volume, but gradually developed and grew larger as the railways expanded.

Timetable Collection

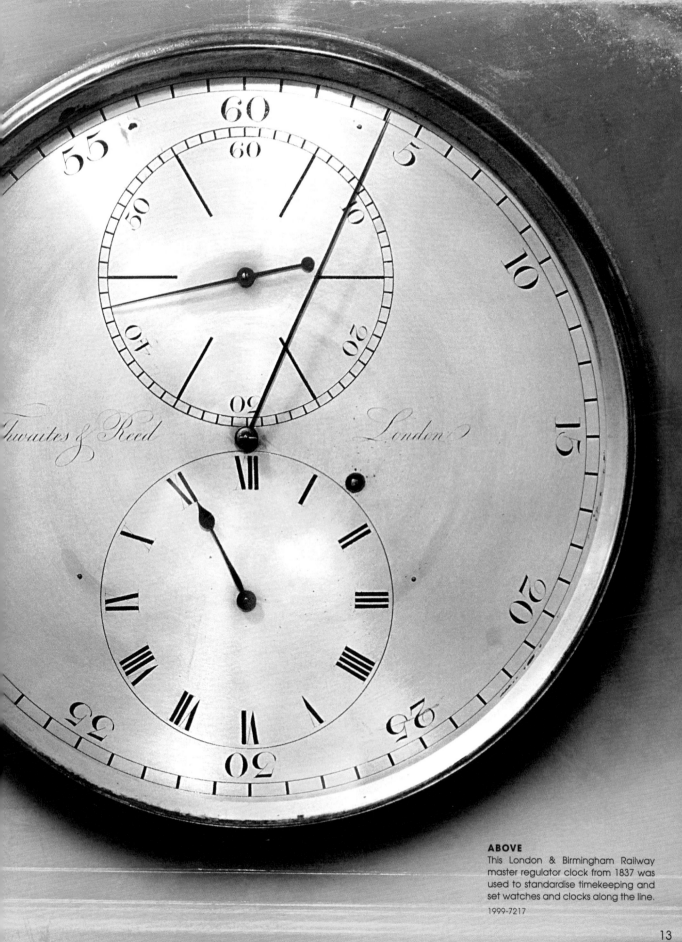

ABOVE
This London & Birmingham Railway
master regulator clock from 1837 was
used to standardise timekeeping and
set watches and clocks along the line.
1999-7217

1833

Brunel's collection of geological specimens

Isambard Kingdom Brunel's engineering genius was based on thorough preparation. A detailed understanding of geology was key to deciding the best route for the Great Western Railway and Brunel chose the right material for the job. The samples in this cabinet carry labels saying where the stone came from and how it might be used.
1977-7952

1834

Bodmin & Wadebridge Railway carriages

These wooden-bodied coaches are rare witnesses to early Victorian travel. Passengers in first class travelled in relative comfort on cushioned seats. However, the carriage wheels were cast iron and frequently broke; on one occasion in 1864 passengers were taken to their destination on the locomotive! The Bodmin & Wadebridge Railway pioneered excursion trains and in April 1840 ran a special service to take passengers to see two murderers hanged at Bodmin Gaol.
1975-7038

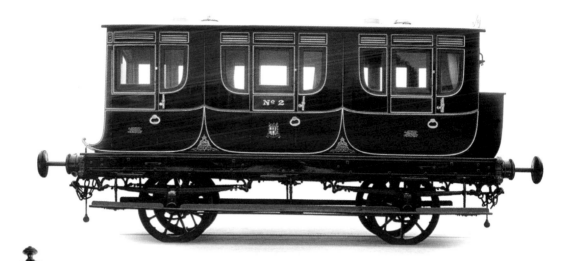

1842

Queen Adelaide's carriage

This is the oldest surviving royal carriage, clearly related in its design to horse-drawn road coaches. It was built for the London & Birmingham Railway in the same year that Queen Victoria became Britain's first monarch to travel by train. However, it was constructed not for her but for Queen Adelaide, Victoria's aunt and the widow of William IV.

1983-7001

1840

Thomas Edmondson's ticket printing machine

Before Thomas Edmondson patented this machine, tickets were cut out by hand. With the new method, a skilled operator could print 200 per minute. The machines' success saw them used around the world and by the 1870s Britain printed more than 500 million tickets in just one year. The last Edmondson press was switched off in 1988, and the use of Edmondson tickets ended a year later.

1869-76

1849

'The Rise and Fall of George Hudson' cartoon

One of the most flamboyant characters of the Railway Mania age of expansion, George Hudson controlled a huge amount of Britain's network and was known as the Railway King. However, his unscrupulous financial dealings led to his downfall and he was satirised mercilessly, as in this cartoon called 'How He Reigned and How He Mizzled'.

2015-7066

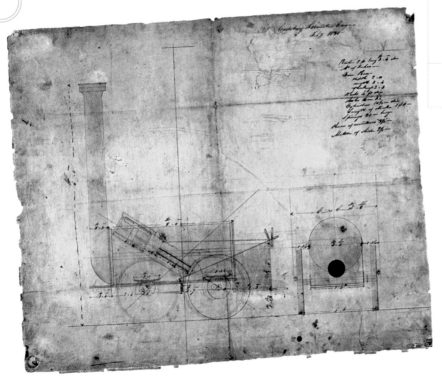

1850

The Robert Stephenson & Company business archives

These documents tell the story of the rise and decline of probably the world's most famous private railway manufacturing firm, Robert Stephenson & Company. It built Rocket and many countries' first locomotives were Stephenson & Co exports. The archive has been selected by UNESCO for its Register of the Memory of the World.

1970-473, 1924-159

1855

Lead shot from the Great Gold Robbery

This bullion box is from the first great train robbery. A shipment of gold was stolen from a guards' van on a South Eastern Railway (SER) train running from London to the south coast, where it met a ferry bound for France. The crime was discovered in Paris, when bank staff realised that thieves on board the train had replaced the gold with lead shot. As a result of the robbery the SER built special bullion vans to avoid carrying gold in guards' vans.

1976-7961

1850

Railway company seals

Before any railway company could exist, Parliament had to pass an Act of Incorporation, which required an official seal. Our collection includes more than 1,600 seals. Some are the only surviving artefacts from companies that have long since ceased to exist. This box holds the seal of the South Yorkshire Joint Line Committee.

1976-7720

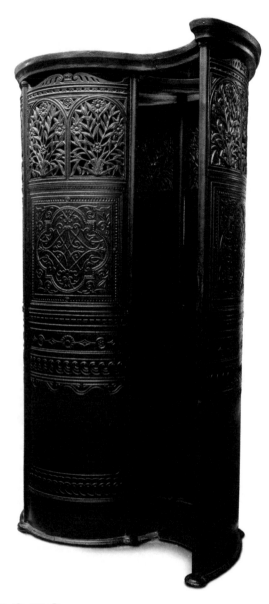

1865

Stationmaster's jacket

This striking stationmaster's jacket is based on the design of a coachman's uniform from the days before the railway. With silver-plated buttons and a velvet collar, it would normally have been worn together with a top hat. It comes from the North Eastern Railway, which took over the pioneering Stockton & Darlington Railway in 1863.

1977-5338

1870

Single stall urinal

Before the 1890s most trains lacked toilets, so providing facilities on station platforms was essential and 'comfort breaks' were built into timetables. This single stall urinal came from Curthwaite station in Cumbria on the Maryport & Carlisle Railway; it may have been made in Glasgow at the Sun Foundry of George Smith and Company, a manufacturer that also produced drinking fountains.

1976-7054

1892

Hardwicke

Competition between railway companies was fierce, and in 1895 the major Anglo-Scottish firms raced between London and Aberdeen in a contest that became known as the Races to the North. Hardwicke took part and on 22 August set a record by running at an average of 67mph over the 141 miles between Crewe and Carlisle. Hardwicke was owned by the London & North Western Railway, and had been built at their workshops in Crewe.

1975-7023

1979-7892

1893

'Going North' by George Earl

This painting shows parties waiting to catch a train at London's King's Cross station to go shooting and fishing in Scotland. A companion painting 'Coming South' depicts the return journey at the end of the shooting season. The images are full of life and detail, and give a good impression of what it was like to travel by train in style during the latter part of the Victorian era.

1990-67

Work and Pleasure

As cities grew and drew their workers from ever further afield, the daily commute became a reality for millions of people. Railways evolved and new lines were built, actively promoting the growth of suburbs and garden cities. For generations, many people's entire lifestyles were only made possible by the railways.

From an early stage, commuter trains were specially designed to carry large numbers of passengers, with doors that enabled them to load and unload quickly. Electric trains, which could accelerate better than those pulled by steam locomotives, increased the speed of commuter services. Signalling was also modernised in the early 20th century to allow more and faster trains to run on suburban lines.

This revolution in so many people's way of life brought commercial opportunities, from bookstalls offering newspapers and magazines for the journey, to new homes within easy reach of the station. Adverts on the railway pushed a multitude of products.

While for many people a train journey is associated with the 'daily grind' of getting to work, the railways have long sought to exploit the opportunities for pleasure travel too, encouraged through cheap tickets, stylish posters and slick publicity. The approach extended beyond pure transport. Popular destinations even had their own railway-owned hotels. Mass travel brought mass holidays, and many of Britain's seaside resorts owe their popularity to the railways' marketing efforts.

ABOVE RIGHT
Before cheap air travel, holidays for many people meant Britain's seaside – and railways promoted the resorts they served. This poster of Bridlington in Yorkshire was designed for the London & North Eastern Railway in 1930 by Henry George Gawthorn.
1986-9043

RIGHT
Big cities could have several important stations. Shown here in about 1949, London's Fenchurch Street was built for the London Tilbury & Southend Railway – a railway that served commuters during the week and people looking for a day out by the sea at weekends.
1995-7233

LEFT
With so many people travelling by train, stations became lucrative places to do business. This stall at Manchester Victoria, photographed in about 1926, sold books, magazines and newspapers.
1997-7059

1900

Electric reading lamp

Before good quality lighting in carriages became standard, you could use this lamp – for a price! Adopted by London's Metropolitan Railway among others, this 'penny-in-the-slot' electric reading light was made by the Railway Automatic Light Syndicate. Thieves often targeted the cash in the machines; a reward of 40 shillings was offered for information that led to conviction.

1916-57

1893

Yellowback novel

Railways created reading time for captive passengers, spawning a whole new genre of affordable, escapist literature that could be read on the train. So-called 'yellowbacks' became known by their cover colour; this one is by the prolific Archibald Clavering Gunter.

2003-7151

1901

Model of a carriage compartment, made for a murder trial

At the turn of the 20th century most carriages had individual compartments that could only be accessed from the platform, which meant passengers were isolated once the train was moving. This model was made for the murder trial of George Parker, who on 17 January 1901 shot and killed farmer William Pearson in a compartment on a London & South Western Railway train. The model was used to demonstrate the layout of the compartment to the jury. Parker was convicted and executed for his crime.

1999-7037

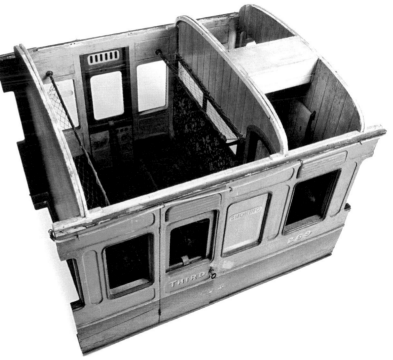

1902

Travelling jewellery case and necklace

This ornate travelling case is inlaid with silver and includes drawers for make-up. It may have belonged to the popular opera singer Adelina Patti (1843–1919). She travelled in her own private railway carriage and had a large house in the Brecon Beacons in Wales.

1986-8022

1912

School of Signalling model railway

Built in 1912 to train staff in the rules of signalling, this layout holds the record as the world's longest continually working model railway. It was made by the Lancashire and Yorkshire Railway and Bassett-Lowke Ltd, and is one of the most complex examples of training railways ever made. It is still used today to train signal staff.

1992-7856

1912

'Letchworth Station' by Spencer Gore

Passengers wait at Letchworth in this post-impressionist oil painting by Camden Town Group painter Spencer Frederick Gore. Letchworth was the world's first Garden City in 1903, but a lack of local employment turned it into one of Britain's first commuter towns. Gore's painting was initially seen as a critique of the railway, but the clean and harmonious composition is now generally interpreted as showing its integration into the landscape.

1983-8607

DINING CARS.

Luncheon, 2/6	Dinner, 3/6
Croute au Pot	Creme Sante
	Turbot Hollandaise
Merlans Portugaise	Chicken Portugaise
Roast Beef	Roast Mutton
Cabbage Potatoes	Peas
	Baked and Boiled Potatoes
Fruit a la Conde	Fruit Tart
	Cheese Salad
Cheese Salad	Ices

FIRST CLASS   13-9-07

The Service of a la Carte Meals is suspended during Table d'Hote

For Tariff see back of Menu

It is particularly requested that no money be paid without a Bill, and that observations and complaints be addressed to Mr Towle, MIDLAND GRAND HOTEL, LONDON, the Bill being enclosed

1914

Midland and Glasgow & South Western joint dining car

With long-distance travel taking many hours, dining facilities for passengers were considered essential. This one was for third class passengers, who would have been kept separate from people travelling first class.

E2009.245.1 1975-7030

1915

London & North Western Railway motor coach

This motor coach was part of an electric train running on the London & North Western Railway's suburban services in London. Electric trains were cleaner than steam trains and accelerated more quickly, making them perfect for moving large numbers of people on lines which had closely spaced stops. Railways serving growing cities were quick to realise this, and the LNWR electrified its London commuter routes decades before its main lines.

1978-7068

1915

Gunpowder van boot

Railways were legally obliged to carry any goods, including hazardous materials. They built specialised vehicles, such as gunpowder vans that were lined with wood to minimise the risk of sparks. Railway workers had to wear special leather overboots with wooden soles. This boot was worn during the First World War when vast quantities of munitions were moved by rail.

1975-704

1915

North Eastern Railway mug from York station

Special buffets were set up at large stations during the First and Second World Wars to cater for soldiers and sailors undertaking often long and difficult journeys: the buffets were staffed by female volunteers. Not all mugs were returned. During the Second World War some were reported to have travelled as far as North Africa.

1997-9298

1915

Clock case from Quintinshill signal box

Britain's worst railway accident was a collision at Quintinshill near Gretna Green, caused by a signalling error on 22 May 1915. Nobody knows exactly how many people died – the official estimate was 227 plus 245 injured, most of them soldiers travelling to war. This Caledonian Railway clock case from the signal box is inscribed on the inside of the door with signallers' signatures from 1916 until the 1960s, plus events surrounding the life of the signal box. What appears to be the first entry reads 'Q'HILL May 22 – 1915'.

1984-7504

1923

Flying Scotsman

Railways were keen to persuade the public they were a fast means of travel and Flying Scotsman's speed exploits make it world-famous. In 1928 the locomotive pulled the inaugural non-stop service from London to Edinburgh and in 1934 it became the first steam locomotive officially to reach 100mph. For its non-stop running, Flying Scotsman was given a corridor tender that allowed the crew to change over between the locomotive and carriages while the train was moving. The locomotive's appearance has altered several times since 1923 and it is shown here with its apple-green London & North Eastern Railway livery and original number, 4472.

2004-7103

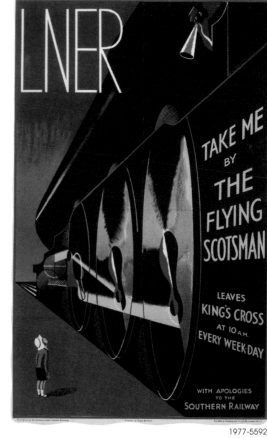

LNER

TAKE ME
BY
THE
FLYING
SCOTSMAN

LEAVES
KING'S CROSS
AT 10 A.M.
EVERY WEEK-DAY

WITH APOLOGIES
TO THE
SOUTHERN RAILWAY

1977-5592

1928

Borough Market Junction signal box

This signal box was said to be the busiest in Britain. At peak times two signallers dealt with 100 trains an hour. It controlled Borough Market Junction in London, where the lines from London Bridge, Cannon Street and Charing Cross converge. It was originally mounted on top of a brick tower that provided a good view over the lines that the signal box controlled.

1991-7211

1929

Karrier Cob

Derived from a three-wheeled dust-cart, the Karrier Cob was adopted by the London, Midland & Scottish Railway. The railway companies built up vast fleets of road vehicles, which they used to deliver goods that had been transported by rail. These little trucks were light, manoeuvrable and gradually took over from horses.

1975-7057

Speed and Style

The poster for the Silver Jubilee service read 'Britain's first streamline train'. It was an advert to define an era, that spoke of speed and glamour beyond what many passengers would experience.

Mallard is famous as the streamlined locomotive that snatched the world steam speed record in 1938. Three years before that, Britain's first streamlined locomotives were used on a train that was fast and glamorous – and looked it. The London & North Eastern Railway (LNER) Silver Jubilee service allowed Newcastle and Darlington businessmen to visit London and return on the same day. The train's design was inspired by the Art Deco style popular at the time, and there were literary connections too; the first engine's name, Silver Link, came from a poem by Sir Walter Scott.

In 1937 the LNER launched the Coronation streamlined service connecting London and Edinburgh. Carriages had double-glazing, an advance on misted-up windows, and 'pressure ventilation', a forerunner of air conditioning. Special sloping-backed observation cars ran at the rear. Passengers were pampered with an at seat service, à la carte food, and a choice of cocktails.

Trains such as the Coronation and the Coronation Scot streamliner of the rival London, Midland & Scottish Railway (LMS), were at the apex of the railway system. They offered luxury symbolic of a service that extended to well-appointed waiting rooms, restaurants and hotels. Yet the railways still made most of their money from humble passenger and freight services, and the era of competing streamlined trains was short-lived, lasting only until the Second World War.

ABOVE RIGHT
Duchess of Hamilton, built by the LMS in 1938. Locomotives like this pulled the Coronation Scot between London and Glasgow.
1976-7000

RIGHT
In 1935, Sir Nigel Gresley created the Silver Jubilee, a train that became a design icon of the 1930s. This poster was produced for the LNER to promote the service, which travelled at an average speed of 67mph.
1975-8398

LEFT
Railways had their own dining ware, which they also used in their hotels and ships. The LNER crockery includes a thistle and rose in its design and was used on its prestigious London–Scotland services.
1996-8035, 1996-8029, 1996-8001, 1996-8048, 1996-8006

1931

Stanton Iron Works
12-ton mineral wagon

Wagons like this kept Britain moving by carrying the coal, iron ore and other minerals so essential for industry, and for domestic cooking and heating. Many of them were privately owned by collieries or merchants, but licensed to run on the railways. This one is known as a five-plank wagon – a reference to the wooden construction of its body.

1978-7115

1931

London & North Eastern Railway
paper fan

Before air conditioning, fans were a useful accessory, and these decorative paper giveaways from the LNER were an early example of targeted advertising. Competition between the railway companies during the inter-war period could be fierce and advertising played a key part in generating custom.

1971-7962

1935

KF Class, number 7

Britain built locomotives for export throughout the world. Many of these locomotives were bigger than those used in Britain. This one was built for use in China by Vulcan Foundry of Newton-le-Willows in Lancashire and was in use for approximately 50 years. It was donated to the museum by the Chinese Government in 1983.

1987-7001

1936

Biscuit tin used to transport 'Live Stock'

As 'common carriers' the railways were expected to transport whatever their clients demanded, which sometimes led to them carrying bizarre cargoes. This tin originally held confectionery, but has had its lid pierced so it could carry live frogs and newts from the Midlands to a secondary school in Swansea. The label shows that the sender paid to have it sent on a passenger train in the care of the guard.

2002-7127

1938

Mallard

Mallard is officially the world's fastest steam locomotive. One of Sir Nigel Gresley's famous A4 engines, it reached over 125mph while pulling a test train on 3 July 1938. The record was achieved on a stretch of line known as Stoke Bank, near Grantham. Gresley was friendly with Ettore Bugatti, the famous car designer who also designed streamlined railcars; it is said that these inspired the curving A4 shape.

1975-7007

1975-7007

1985-8908

1977-5851

1939–1945

Wartime posters and artwork

During the Second World War the railways produced posters to publicise the war effort, emphasising that the movement of troops and military supplies took precedence over passenger trains (bottom left). From June 1940 the increased risk to coastal shipping led to transport by sea being heavily cut back, with much of the freight transferred to rail. Blackouts became common from 1940 and public information posters reminded passengers of safe practice when alighting from trains (bottom right). As railway workers were called up to fight, more and more women replaced men in certain roles on the railways such as porters (top right) and the cleaning of locomotives (top left).

All Clear for the Guns
ON
BRITISH RAILWAYS

1979-7909

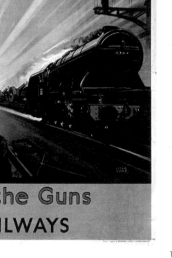

LOOKOUT
FOR THE PLATFORM

Before alighting in the blackout
Make sure the train is in the station
Make sure you are on the
platform side of the train

BRITISH RAILWAYS
G.W.R.   L.T.   L.N.E.R   SR   LMS

1978-9873

1944

J P Richards'
scale-model collection

There are 610 models in the James Peel Richards collection, recognised by Guinness World Records as the largest collection of model railway vehicles made by one person. Born in 1902, Richards started making models in 1944 and continued until shortly before his death in 1999. All the O Gauge fine scale models represent vehicles running on the London & North Western Railway between 1902 and 1923.

1999-7392

1998-10951

1951

EM1 26020

People in post-war Britain were increasingly unwilling to work in the dirty conditions created by steam locomotives, but when this EM1 electric was displayed at the 1951 Festival of Britain, steam engines were still being built in their hundreds. The London & North Eastern Railway had built a similar locomotive in 1941, but the plan to electrify the Sheffield to Manchester Woodhead Route was delayed by the Second World War. Even today much of the main line railway network has not been electrified.

1978-7005

1944

Wireless set from Montgomery's saloon

In the run-up to D-Day and the liberation of Europe in 1944, commander of the Allied ground forces Field Marshal Bernard Law Montgomery listened to this radio, which was housed in the saloon car of a train created for his use. The train was given the codename Rapier.

1986-8050

1949

Laddie

Laddie was an Airedale terrier. With a box strapped to his back he collected money for the Southern Railway Servants Orphanage and worked at Wimbledon and Waterloo stations between 1946 and 1949. He retired in 1956. After Laddie's death he returned to Wimbledon, stuffed and mounted in a glass case. He continued to raise money until 1990.

1990-7629

1955

The world's longest station sign

This sign, on the maroon background of British Railways' London Midland Region, measures 19 feet 3 inches (5.9 metres) long when all its three pieces are put together. The station is on Anglesey and opened in 1848. The name means 'The Church of St Mary in a hollow of white hazel, near to a rapid whirlpool, and to St Tysilio's Church near to a red cave'. The name was actually invented in the 1860s to encourage tourism, and it worked!

1986-8670

1955

Diesel-electric Deltic prototype

The Deltic was a gamble by the private English Electric Company which hoped that fast and powerful diesel locomotives would prove an attractive alternative to expensive railway electrification. This Deltic was a prototype, but 22 locomotives were built in 1961–2 to take over from steam on express trains such as The Flying Scotsman and to offer the first services regularly running at 100mph.

1963-80

1960

Evening Star

Evening Star was the last steam locomotive built for British Railways at the works in Swindon. The name was chosen through a competition for workers. Although a heavy freight locomotive, Evening Star was painted in the full green livery normally applied to express passenger engines, rather than the normal plain black. It was also given a Great Western Railway-style copper cap to its chimney. Yet Evening Star only worked for about five years, and by 1968 all of British Rail's main line steam locomotives had been replaced by diesel or electric vehicles.

1975-7024

NDROBWLLLLANTYSILIOGOGOGOCH

1962

Scissors used by Dr Beeching to open Plymouth station

These scissors were used by British Railways chairman Dr Richard Beeching in 1962 to open the modernised Plymouth station. While Dr Beeching has gone down in history for very different 'cuts' – slashing the size of the nation's railway through line closures – he also presided over important modernisation to areas including inter-city passenger services and freight.

2008-7162

1965

British Rail logo

In 1965 a corporate rebranding saw British Railways re-launched as British Rail and created the famous 'double arrow' logo that is still used today. The revamp extended to trains, ships, silver and ceramic ware, stationery, uniforms and signage. This enamelled sign is from the façade of Bristol Temple Meads station, while the page from the corporate identity manual shows the strict guidelines for station signposting.

1999-7716

Station signposting M.O.T. Direction sign		sheet no.	3/504
		issued	May 1965

All dimensions expressed as stroke widths of capital letter.

1	General	This sign has been accepted by the Ministry of Transport and will be included in later issues of the Road Traffic Signs Regulations. No variants on this sign are permitted. Where any other wording, such as, 'Marylebone Station', 'Freight Depot', 'Motorail Terminal', 'Car Ferry', is required, the standard M.o.T. signs are to be used, without the British Rail symbol.
2	Siting	For guidance on siting refer to M.o.T. Traffic Signs Manual, H.M.S.O. 1965.
3	Size	The overall size of the sign depends on the size of lettering required for the particular site. Normally a suitable x-height would be 2" or 3" but 1½" may be used where signs are directed at pedestrian traffic.
4	Layout	Lettering to be M.o.T. Transport Heavy. For accurate setting-out of British Rail symbol see sheet 1/05. Symbol to be centred vertically on panel. Lowercase to line through with horizontal lines of symbol.
5	Colour	Lettering and chevron – black on white. Border – blue B.S.2660 No. 0.013. Symbol – white on B.R. Flame Red rectangle. Grey for posts, fittings and backs of signs – B.S.2660 No. 9.101.
6		Full size prints may be obtained from the Chief Architect B.R.B., Chief Publicity Officer or Director of Industrial Design.

Innovations

In the 1970s British Rail needed to change its tired image, tarnished by decay and line closures, so it created a train that became a household name: the Inter-City 125. Otherwise known as the High Speed Train (HST), it cut journey times – and tickets were kept at reasonable prices too.

Britain's new diesel trains were part of the nationalised railway's answer to rising car ownership and new motorways. The HST first carried passengers in 1976, only eight years after British Rail ran its last main line steam locomotives and when 1960s cutbacks under Dr Richard Beeching were still a recent memory.

The HST would become one of the most successful train designs ever, but it was a compromise because Britain wanted high speed without the dedicated lines that were built in Japan and France. So British Rail created the world's fastest diesel train, able to run on the existing network without even needing electrified lines. It was an approach that typified the value for money improvements of the 1970s and 1980s.

British Rail's plan had always been for something even more radical – an Advanced Passenger Train (APT). The project developed technologies still used today, like tilting which allowed the train to go faster through curves. However, a series of technical and political problems led to the project being abandoned in the 1980s.

In 1994 there was a major breakthrough which heralded the railways' imminent resurgence. That year the Channel Tunnel opened, a 31.5 mile/50.7km line under the seabed which directly linked Britain and the Continent of Europe for the first time in 8,500 years.

TOP LEFT
The Advanced Passenger Train pioneered technologies that are in common use today, but the project itself was abandoned in the 1980s.
DS140215-103615

TOP RIGHT
Since the Channel Tunnel opened, passengers can travel direct from London to Paris or Brussels. Opened in 1868, St Pancras has gained a new life as Britain's main international station.
DF110138-91585

RIGHT
British Rail backed up its launch of new High Speed Trains with a marketing campaign to attract people from their cars. This poster from 1979 advertised Inter-City services between York and London.
1979-7842

Inter-City 125

Have a good trip!

*Fastest journeys.

1972

High Speed Train (HST)

As car ownership increased, British Rail needed something to attract passengers. The answer was the High Speed Train – also known as the Inter-City 125 due to its top speed of 125mph. With a diesel-powered engine, the HST did not need expensive electrification at a time of little support for the railways. This prototype power car was a test vehicle for what became the world's fastest diesel train. After many years out of use it was restored to working order in 2014.

1988-7000

1978

Shinkansen bullet train

For many years engineers tried to develop faster trains for existing routes, but Japan took a radical new approach. In 1964, the Shinkansen – or bullet train – had its own purpose-built lines. Initially trains reached 130mph/209kmh and speeds have progressively increased. High speed lines have since been widely adopted elsewhere. This vehicle is from the original Series 0 design. It was donated to the museum by the West Japan Railway Company in 2001.

2001-7500

2002-7143

1989

Channel Tunnel muck truck locomotive

Before 1994, crossing the English Channel involved travelling by boat or flying. The Channel Tunnel physically connected Britain's railway to the Continent for the first time and brought to fruition an idea that had been around at least since the time of Napoleon. The project also led eventually to the opening of Britain's first dedicated high-speed line, the Channel Tunnel Rail Link or High Speed 1. This Hunslet locomotive was used in the tunnel's construction, pulling the muck trucks which removed the spoil.

1992-7394

2007

High Speed 1 leaflet

London's St Pancras International station opened in 2007. The grand, refurbished Victorian terminus connects Britain with Europe – it is only 2 hours 15 minutes to Paris by Eurostar. The 68 miles of new railway to the channel tunnel is High Speed 1 – Britain's first new main line in a century and the first designed for truly high speed travel. Eurostar services have a maximum speed of 186mph.

2008-7057

The National Collection

Britain's National Collection is one of the greatest in the world – and that brings its own challenges. The National Railway Museum is the custodian of objects ranging from letters and tickets, photographs and large paintings, to locomotives weighing over 100 tonnes.

In all, the National Collection contains more than 2 million objects, over 250 of which are vehicles such as locomotives and carriages. In contrast, there are an estimated 1.75 million photographs including official pictures taken by the railway companies, and the collections of gifted enthusiastic amateurs. We have buttons and books, posters and porters' barrows, signals and sections of track.

Managing such a huge and varied collection is a major task, especially as it is truly national; not all of our collection is housed at York or Shildon. At any one time, around 2,500 objects will be loaned out to museums and railways around the country. For example, many are displayed at STEAM, the Museum of the Great Western Railway in Swindon.

Many of the loaned objects are on static display, but others can be operated and demonstrated to the public. Most of these are locomotives, and we have a number that are either in working condition or being restored for operation by our partners around the country. In the early days of the museum such loans tended to be of steam locomotives but they now include historic diesels as well, right up to the power car for the prototype High Speed Train.

LEFT
Flying Scotsman, photographed in 2011 with the number 502, undergoing restoration in the workshop of Ian Riley's & Son Ltd in Bury.
DF111138

National Railway Museum Leeman Road York YO2 4XJ Telephone 0904 21261
Official opening 27 September 1975 An outstation of The Science Museum London

ABOVE
Welding a crack on one of the horn boxes during the Flying Scotsman restoration in 2011.
DF111467

ABOVE RIGHT
The official opening poster for the National Railway Museum in September 1975.
2000-7803

Our links are international. Objects have come to York on loan from overseas museums, while artefacts from the National Collection have been to North America, Asia, and Continental Europe. Stephenson's Rocket has made it as far as Japan.

A large collection such as ours needs constant attention, and we have a continuous programme of conservation and restoration. Some is done in-house, but given the specific skills needed by the diversity of artefacts in our care, much is undertaken by outside specialists working under careful supervision. Many of the smaller objects are fragile, and before any work starts we need to decide whether to conserve the artefact in its current state, or restore it to the condition it had at a significant stage in its history. The right answer will vary from object to object.

A recent high-profile acquisition has been a section of wooden track from the 18th century, Willington Waggonway, a key forerunner of the railways that followed. This was discovered during excavations alongside the River Tyne and, like the famous Tudor warship Mary Rose, has had to undergo a period of careful conservation before being put on display.

Not all the objects we care for on behalf of the nation are very old. Railways do not stand still, and neither must we. We continue to collect to enhance our understanding of the early days of railways right up to the present day. A modern marvel of engineering joined the collection

in 2015, when Eurostar donated a power car from one of the trains that speeds through the Channel Tunnel and across the UK, France and Belgium at up to 186mph.

Smaller than either of these, but no less significant, is a complete collection of parliamentary papers covering the period from the early railways through to 1906 – a phenomenally important historical resource documenting the rise of railways, which includes drawings, maps, plans and personal testimony.

At York, the museum maintains the Search Engine archive and library where documents, books and photographs from the collection are made available for research. The archive is open at certain times of the week for people simply to drop in. We also have an active educational programme aimed at schools and colleges, and collaborate with higher education establishments. These include the University of York with which we jointly run the Institute of Railway Studies, and the University of Birmingham's Centre of Railway Research.

As the railways continue their own journey, our aim is to make sure a visit to the museum is as exciting and relevant for future visitors as it has ever been since we opened in 1975. We have new plans for the display of objects in the Great Hall and to create a more immersive, interactive experience explaining the great changes railways have made to people's lives over the last 200 years.

ABOVE
In Search Engine you can access original material from our archives, research railway topics and find answers to your railway-related questions.

Supporters

Thank you for your donation

We would like to thank all our visitors, who have shown tremendous generosity by donating on their visits to us. We are now raising in excess of £500,000 a year in visitor donations.

Become a Patron – invest in our future

As a Patron you will be at the heart of the museum, enjoying our world class hospitality and intellectual resources. Patrons have exclusive access to Britain's National Collection and our expert curatorial staff, as well as a tailor-made programme of events and dinners.

Your annual patronage makes a real difference to our work, ensuring we are able to tell the story of the railways. Your support helps us to inspire the next generation and influence the way people connect with the National Railway Museum now and in the future. There has never been a more exciting time to become a Patron of the National Railway Museum. Patronage levels start at just £500 a year.

For more details contact
The National Railway Museum,
Development Team,
Leeman Road, York YO26 4XJ.
Tel: 01904 685774.
development@nrm.org.uk

A gift in your will – a lasting legacy

Leaving a gift in your will to The National Railway Museum is the most personal, precious and lasting contribution anyone can make. Any gift, large or small, will help to ensure that the museum can educate and delight visitors for generations to come.

Get involved – become an volunteer

Investing your time and energy is very important to us and we welcome all to our volunteering programme, whatever your background or experience. Volunteers help out in all areas of the Museum, gaining invaluable hands-on experience, and are critical to ensuring we can offer the most to our visitors. You don't even need to be in York, as you can help with some projects, like cataloguing, online.

Contact us at volunteer.nrm@nrm.org.uk

We are grateful for the support from all of our funders including:
Abellio Group
Alstom
Ambersphere
Angel Trains Ltd
Arriva UK Trains Ltd
Arup Group Ltd
Bachmann Industries Europe Plc
Bombardier Transportation UK Ltd
Colas Rail
Dellner Ltd
East Coast
ESG
Eversholt Rail Ltd
First Great Western
First TransPennine Express
GHD
Grand Central Railway Company Ltd
Hornby plc
Mechan Limited
Network Rail LNE
Northern Rail
NSARE
Omnicom Engineering Ltd
Porterbrook
Rail Media Group
REPTA
Ryder Architecture
Science City York
Shepherd Group
Thales UK
Anonymous NRM Donors
Arts Council England
Heritage Lottery Fund Yorkshire
The National Archives
Branch Line society
Friends of the National Railway Museum
Rotary Club of Jarrow with Harton
The Sylvia and Colin Shepherd Charitable Trust
Yorventure Environmental Body Ltd
NRM Patrons